He Waited For ME!

By Anthony Boyd

Copyright 2020 by Anthony Boyd
All rights reserved

No part of this book may be reproduced in any format without the author and publisher's permission.

December 2020

Printed and bound in the United States of America

ISBN 979-857-1686372

He Waited for ME!
By Anthony Boyd

Also available on Amazon Kindle

Dedication

Special thanks goes out to My Pastor and Godly influence in the things that pert ain to Jesus Christ. Pastor Bessie Terry.

Introduction
Anthony Boyd

It is my strongest desirer that this book helps someone. The Spirit of the Living God spoke to me one day.

God Said to me, "You were cast down but you were not utterly destroyed. I held you in the palm of my hand!"

It came through so strong I knew it was God. I got out my Bible to confirm it. I found this text Psalm 37:23,24 '7he steps of a good man are ordered by the LORD: and he dellghteth in his way. Though he fall, he shall not be utterly cast down: for the LORD upholdeth him with his hand.

This has been my inspiration my whole life. The draw of the lord has been so strong in my life. Even in my darkest days I could not out run the draw of His love and His Unwillingness to never, ever give up on me *He Waited for Me*. He is waiting on you to totally submit to His will and purpose for your Life. Do be inspired to come forth. Allow the things you have been through to launch you forward into your destiny. He is waiting for you.

Genesis

There are too many factures to number that contributed to you turning out to be the person that you are. These are the things that lead to me being the broken person that I became. These are the things that lead to me being broken at the feet for Jesus and fully surrendered. I wish they could all be good but they are not. You, as well as myself, have had our hands forced to deal with things we would rather not have. We did the best we knew with what we had been exposed to. Hey we tried and in some instants we failed. Trial and Error without a solid mentor has educated us. I'm not proud of the lessons I've learned in life, but I do value every lesson learned. Life's best lessons are not always learned under the best circumstances. Here is a shot in the dark. These are things I've learned. Maybe I can prevent you from learning some of the hardest lessons I've learned the way I learned them at least.

Have you ever asked yourself the question? What has contributed to you being the way that you are? I would have to ask what would it be? I think at an early age I was exposed to a lot of wrong stuff (imagery). I have a very vivid memory even from a very early age. One thing that I consider a hindrance is I was exposed to enormous amounts of perversion. I have a very vivid memory. I remember little things even as an infant. I remember being a small baby and my mother and father holding me on my grandmother's front porch. I remember my aunt (my mother ' s sister came to stay with us in NY and babysitting. I had to have been less than 3 years old.

I recall my earliest intake of (imagery).. I was 10 years old when I had my first encounter with pornographic images. It was at my grandmother's house one summer. There was an old barn. My uncle had a hidden stash of adult magazines. That first image was forever sealed in my young mind. It was a nude lady standing on a bar with men sitting around the bar. Their eyes were fixed eye level on her intimate private parts, as she squatted and urinated in a cocktail glass. Just to much of virgin eyes!

Home Life

There was never a sense of love expressed in my home. The words "I love you" were never spoken. There was no nurturing in my home. Only thing that brought attention to yourself was misbehaving. Mother and father always seemed to be at odds with each other. Tension was always in the air. This was in the mid 70's. The New York school systems were in an experimenting phase. It allowed the kids to choose what they wanted to be taught. I chose cooking every time. I got left behind. I was in the third grade but could not read. I was a terrible kid but it wasn't my fault. Outside influences were very strong. I became part of gang active and physical violence. I fought everyday There was never a day I went to school and not have to fight. My parents did take a stab at getting me help to read. They hired a Muslim family that taught me to read. The New York school system was failing me miserably.

Who's the Man?

My daddy made the decision for us to move to North Carolina but he stayed back in New York for 4 years. I felt like I was the man of the house. Finally, he moved to North Carolina. I believe it was after four years.

He took over his role as head of the house. He never told me "Thank you." I was feeling some internal emotions about this thing. He made me submit to him when he disciplined me. He broke my spirit. Alpha male was reduced back to the little boy again.

Often time's single moms call their small sons their "little man". He made me call him daddy. He didn't really nurture me as a father figure. In his defense, I don' t think he knew how. Maybe he didn't want the role at all. He was raised without a father and maybe he was thinking he turned out fine.

When I was 12 years old my mother made him start taking me with him. She told him she couldn't teach me to be a little boy ultimately a man. I think he resented it at first. Maybe it was the fact she told him he was obligated to do it. The fact she told him to do it may have been difficult for him to comprehend. I believe he resented it at first because I was eyes and ears on everything he did.

He quickly trained me in the art of infidelity. Oh or so I thought at the time he was the first one to teach me infidelity. But, it was only when I was much older I realized different, I'm talking adulthood, that I determined it was my mother who taught me, first. All the years we used to visit North Carolina; my mom had a boyfriend down south.

I didn't realize it was wrong until I had deep reflections on my childhood memories. All my life I had resentment for my daddy making me keep secrets about his open affection to his girlfriends in my presence

My mom was just as guilty and was "playing church".

Every summer we returned back to NY after we spent the summer in North Carolina. She was being one way at church but living a very deceptive life.

Therefore, I coined this saying, "living a discreet, hidden, and secretive lifestyle is not living Holy unto God!"

Some people think they are better than other people. This is because some people's personal struggles and growth has been more public than others. Living a

Closet Christian life style does not allow you to elevate yourself in your own mind above others. Pride always comes before a fall. You may not have experienced the same failings someone else has. Bur, it does not make you better. A Christian that masquerades themselves as living or leading a Concealed sinful life is just as twisted. They are no better than the individual who struggles and has been exposed publicly. Living a discreet (concealed Sinful) life is not living Holy as God requires. Being discreet about your sin is not living Holy!

Transforming from Bad to Worse

Corporal punishment in NC school system finally got me somewhat settled. I make note that of three times in my life I can recall extreme amounts of debilitating perversion. First, when I was 15 years old my father friends gave me vocal lessons on (self-pleasuring) masturbation. They talked about it as if it was a rite of passage to manhood. They talked often very compassionately about it.

I explored the possibilities of this practice. It was very addictive at first. I didn't have access to pornographic material. I generated my own motivation by perverted imagery that had already been sealed in my mind. I got at good at creating images and I used them to create wet dreams while I slept.

The mind is very powerful we must guard our minds entry points; what we see, what we hear and what we ponder on as our desires of our hearts.

Second, I knew a guy that was a friend of my father's. He was the first person I knew who had a satellite dish and he recorded porn. Now watch how Satan works. Satan will supply the things that can lead to your personal demise and broken relationship with God. This can be done without any out of pocket expense. Joe was my friend. He allowed me to keep as many tapes as I wanted for free. Really, they were not free they were costing me personal depravity.

This is when I really had the hooks set in me for pornographic material. I was watching a tape and the imagery was so vivid and intense. There were so many sex acts. It got me so stirred I ejaculated on myself. Do you see the progression of going from bad to worse? I went from self-motivated stimulation to just watching a tape that could make me achieve the same climax. After this, I looked for every opportunity to watch pornographic material.

Third, I use to work with a guy that was a master in perversion. He had literally hundreds of movies. They were black market movies. You couldn't just get this stuff anywhere. There were tapes with; homosexual sexual images, bestiality, self-mutilation that was being accompanied with sexual acts. This imagery held my interest for a season

Even before the my VCR broke, it dawned on me when you are addicted to pornographic material. it is a crippling addiction. It has the potential to destroy your life. Your partner cannot and will not live up to those perverted fantasies you get off those tapes. So, a person hooked on pornographic material will spend unhealthy amounts of time only pleasuring themselves. That is not want God intended. The VCR got broken and I got drawn to God. I put it in the shop for repairs. Every time I went back it was not fixed yet. I ended up rededicating my life back to God. I was drawn to the God who touched me in my youth.

The Fallout

Bad decisions are always accompanied with fallout or consequences. All that imagery that I took in the Satan would bring it up from time to time. I feel he does this to tempt you and to see where you are spiritually. Satan checks to see if you are truly delivered. Satan makes you have flash backs. Often times and seasons they are very strong. Your tools are as follows; bind the Spirit of lust, rebuke his influences, chastening of your flesh and remove yourself from that which has a strong pull on you. If you are married make for certain you gear all your sexual affections towards your spouse. Keep in the front of your mind God permits the pleasing of the flesh with your spouse, Only!

Marriage is honorable in all and the bed undefiled. I realize regular opportunities to ravish your spouse helps to keep everything intact. Anything Satan tries to tempt you with concerning your intimacy outside the home, is a trick. You can get what you need inside the home and it will be blessed

Save a Little of You for You!

I have experienced a lot of hurt and truthfully. I have dished out some hurt. But, maybe you can relate to this. I have at times given so much in relationships with absolutely nothing to show for it. I have put out financially, spiritually, morally, co-signed, helped raised, and adopted. All this was done without a thank you. I never try to come across super spiritual. Sometimes telling your testimony you can be over the top with Christianese. For me this is a true statement, "{All broken roads lead me back to Jesus!} " In the way of relationships, I have failed terribly.

I picked. I chose one failed relationship after another. It started with my very first relationship was destined for failure. She and I were the same age, but from the first kiss I knew she had experience in somethings I hadn't. She probably had a skill set beyond my years. I always tried to obligate her to be faithful. I consistently tried to intimidate her into being exclusive to just it being us. I attempted to convenience her it could always be she and I against the world.

This was a heavy mantle for a pair of 16-year olds! I would always hear rumors about things she may have been doing contrary to a committed relationship. I always thought she had a slick side (deceptive) about her. I would always ignored the rumors and made excuses for her. I thought I was in love and I learned a fatal skill even then. I turned a blinded eye to things that were obvious and made excuses because I loved her.

Never make excuses for people you love. IF they are wrong they are wrong. If you make excuses, it will come back and bite you. They will try to use it to manipulate and control you with that practice. I know now that being in love with a person is not beneficial to you unless it is 100% mutual. If I hadn't mention it already this was my first failed relationship.

On to the Next One

I tried to figure out what went wrong. This was the first relationship I gave my all. It didn't end well. I caught her in a compromising position with another guy. There was an altercation that I almost went to jail. It ended in violence.

So, what did I invest in this young lady? I showed her: to be highly aware of her self- worth, to be independent, to be self-motivated and how to exceed her own expectations. In other words, I trained her to not need me or rely on no one else.

It worked! She started to achieve. She got a new job, new car and a new life without me. The best way to get over a person you were in a relationship with is simple they say. This is what they call a rebound person or (on to the next one.) This person helps you come back from a serious relationship disconnect.

This is trouble! You end up committing to a person you don't know well at all. They just happen to be filling a void because you are wounded. They just filling a hollow place left by the last person. You don't really care about being around them all that much. They are just something to do. They can't fill the place of that person you really loved and would have given your life for.

The Cycle

My first wife starts a cycle. Cycle- a series of events that are regularly repeated in the same order. From day one she kept hounding me about being her husband but she was the only one filling a void. We were compatible absolutely on no levels. She was totally a big kid. She was very spoiled brat. We didn't' t have a mode of communication. She was embarrassing in public. She would publicly display fits of rage when she couldn't get her way. Extreme manipulation she expressed at all times. They never did anything to support our cause. They were the full expression of dead weight. There is a R & B song with the lyrics, "I can do bad by myself I don't need on help to starve to death.". This was true for me. I never thought in my adulthood that I would be hungry and not know where my next meal was coming from.

I experienced this with her. To add insult to injury she was never faithful and never contributed or brought anything to the table. I did find out she was making money. This was by accident. I overheard a conversation she had with her girlfriend. She was prostituting at the job she had with the hospital. She said she was getting paid $ 250 dollars a pop.

I couldn't phantom in my natural mind who would pay her $250. She was working there after she had HER first child. Somethings in life you just know. After 3 days of this marriage, I knew it was going to end up on a trash heap. The fact of the matter is I was drunk when I did my vows. I was so immature then.

Round 2

Here I go again with this vicious cycle. This in keeping with the notion of getting over someone with the next person. It is insane. I was already on the slippery slope even before I was officially divorced. I was making these bad choices. I chose these bad relationships. Here I go again with wife number two. She was night and day from the first wife. She respected me. She valued what I had to say. She appreciated the things I did. She backed me financially. At first, she loved spending time with me. She changed her lifestyle to fit mine. This relationship prospered. We had homes, and nice automobiles. I was a daddy and a child supporter to her two children. I did this for four years.

The kids chose to move out with their daddy. This was when I became the mental health specialist because that move brought their mom to an all-time low. I was a full-time nurturer. At that point, I tried to gird them up to keep them from having a nervous breakdown.

Here I go again trying to invest, build up and remake or make over somebody else. I did not realize it then but I do now. I did not possess any stability myself to keep trying to build other people.

The most important part of any home is the foundation. I definitely did not have a good foundation. My home life and my family at best was a dysfunctional family. I now know every relationship is dysfunctional unless it is founded on Jesus Christ. Christ is the solid rock I stand. All other ground is sinking sand.

This relationship lasted for many years. This sounds so far as recovery. I could probably end here with we lived happily ever after. We were serving God. Yes, I was saved. I founded a church and was a Pastor for years. I was walking in the Call upon my Life. I did so the best I knew in pleasing God.

For a Season

In the book of Matthew Satan tempted Jesus in the wilderness. Jesus overcame Satan. The bible says a very noteworthy thing. Satan departed for a season. He will always come back to tempt you again and again. My story does not end with things just going well. There came times when I would be struck with an illness that would take me off the scene three months at a time. The doctors had no explanation at all. I would experience vomiting every day to the point where there was nothing in me. I would be throwing up bowel. I would not be able to keep anything down and would have extreme weight lost. It was during one of these times the Satan would wage war in my head daily. I would roll around in the floor most of the day with stomach pain. I would be alone. I didn't know why I was alone because I had a wife. I was married. Anything you go through is much better when it is someone there. Prior to becoming sick, I begged my wife to spend more time with me. They had jobs away from home which didn't require her to stay away as much as they did. I found myself extremely lonely. I was in a new home, with new cars and married. The devil was setting me up with being lonely. I had stuff. I had a luxury sports car, motorcycle and a new truck. Yet I was lonely and the stuff couldn't feel the void. The crux of the matter was, I was lonely, Yes! The biggest void is I had slipped in my relationship with the Lord.

The Trap

If you ever get to the place that you do not learn from your mistakes, failure comes. The fall comes. If you fail to learn from your mistakes, Satan does! He plans new strategies based on your same old mistakes. One day while I was sick a co-worker came by to see me. When she left she told me she loved me. Those were the words I had been missing. They sparked a feeling in me I had been missing. The trap was set. I was struggling with what to name this section. I could have just implied that I fell into a situation accidentally.

Because of that, these next few chapters are going to be dark, disappointing, desperate, and depressing. These things are a result of open rebellion against God. There is a formula that leads to personal pursuit of self-destruction. This is the pattern of behavior that will get you there.

I was a Pastor who lost sight of what was really important. My focus became on my image. I wanted to look the role as a successful Pastor. I had the big SUV, luxury sports sedan, big truck, and the top American brand favorite motorcycle.

These were all to fill a bigger void. I was extremely lonely and there had grown distance between Jesus and I. It was a gap that I created. I failed in spending time with the Lord and His Word. I was busy with ministry. I didn't take time to allow myself to be nourished by his presence or the fullness of the power of His Word. I would search the scriptures for messages. I would search the scriptures to accommodate a need that would arise for members. I was consistently giving out of myself. I never refilled. I never found anyone to talk with when I felt spiritually weak, physically weak, vulnerable, or even tempted. I allowed myself to be pressed with so many things.

Not Sticky

I tried to be the glue for trying to maintain/sustain relationships that were odd in nature.   These are some examples. I had brothers I grew up with. Then I had a half-brother and a half - sister. I met the sister about a year before my father passed. They weren't communicating. I was constantly relaying messages and having to justify why they weren't communicating with each other.

Then, I had kids that were not mine. I was trying to measure up to being a good dad. I had a grandfather of my father that I only met at my father's grave site. I was attempting to keep this awkward relationship going.

Finally, I said, "To Much!"

I started question myself as to, "Why did I have to do right all the time?"

At this time, I made the decision, "I'm going to do me!" Therein lies the course of personal pursuit of self-destruction.

Now, back to my great fall: I'm in a place where I am better accomplishing *My Personal Pursuit of Self-destruction.*

Let me get back to the story about the co- worker.

After that day, she, the co-worker, would tell me she loved me every time we would have conversation. She said she thought it was important to tell me because I meant a lot to her over the fifteen years we had worked together. We had conversation over some deep inter -personal topics over the years. We had discussed our needs, fears and expectations in every area of our lives. During the course of years, we discussed our physical, emotional, spiritual, and sexual needs. We were actually tied in more than we knew. We had developed what I know now to be a communion of souls or a (Soulish Tie). This is very dangerous to any relationship if you have this bond outside your relationship with your spouse. Due to extended hours of conversation we knew that we could fulfill each other's needs.

Soul Searching

I thought the problem was I was lonely. I thought the problem was I didn't have at home a wife that would cater to my needs. The problem was actually simple. I had strayed away from God and wouldn't yield to His voice. I yielded to the voices of; myself (flesh), Satan had managed to ignite what was bad inside of me, in this case. You see, I have been knowing the voice of God ever since I was A little Child.

The voice speaking was definitely not God. You see I was listening to myself (flesh), Satan and outside influences were so loud they drowned out the voice of the Holy Spirit.

When all is said and done, at the end of the day, you could probably say my fall was calculated. It was weighed out. Instead of a fall it was another personal pursuit of self-destruction.

I gave into my flesh and permitted the relationship to become physical. I became twisted at this point. All I wanted was to make this co-worker happy at any cost. I failed the church. I turned my back on God. I refused to do the mandate, the mission, the calling, and ministry for my life. I created public shame.

Truthfully, I wanted wife number two to hurt because at that time I felt she left me vulnerable. I was very angry at her. That was pride speaking. No one else made me do anything. I still had the choice to do right. My desires overruled His purpose for my life. Certainly, you can visualize how foolish this sounds.

It was a risk I took that almost cost me my life. I was ashamed and embarrassed. I wouldn't' look at myself in the mirror. Early on I sought professional help. I felt a little better about myself. During this season, Jesus kept pulling at my heart to just walk away from this situation and come back to Him.

I was too stubborn. This was a mess. I acknowledged this was solely my mess and bad decision. I decided I was going to make it work.

The Lord constantly puts people in our path to remind us who you are in Him and the calling, mandate, mission and ministry that is supposed to be in your life. He sent people to counsel me in some of the most unexpected times and places. I remember one old Baptist preacher was in a class I was teaching in the secular world. He come and sit down beside me.

He asked me, "What is on my mind?"

I said, "Friends and family have abandoned me."

He said, "There isn't anything you have done that hasn't been done before."

And he shared, "Whatever you have done would probably be done again by someone else."

He declared unto me, "The Lord will give you new friends and family."

This blessed me when I needed it. I would get temporary relief from time to time. Still the shame, guilt, embarrassment, and depression became stronger.

Silencing God

There were still fruitless efforts of me attempting to silence the voice of God. The medicine of choice was alcohol. I drank alcohol every day. I drank continually but often times still remained sober. I couldn't even get drunk.

Then one day the Spirit of Suicide showed up. He was there to stay to cause me by my own hand to abort the plan of God for my life. He wanted me stone cold dead. He would not leave me alone.

I started to try to get back to going to church. I guess I was hoping someone would see I was in deep an in spiritual trouble. No one did.

I would attempt to have conversation with the pastor of the church I was attending. I was there for a year. I never could. I guess he was too busy to be concerned for my soul. Hey, I won't mad at him. I would go to church services and return to my truck. The Spirit of Suicide would be there waiting, sitting on the passenger seat.

I finally, made up my mind. I was such an embarrassment to the Lord. No one would ever listen to me again. I had messed up too bad for God to use me ever again. I was going to end my life. I knew when, where, and how I was going to do it. I guess I contemplated telling someone. Actually, murder-suicide was in play in my head.

Then I started thinking about failures. I was going to take out the person I thought helped me get to this mess. I was angary at myself for getting to this desperate, deep, dark and depressed place. I opened the laptop on the kitchen table. It was on a social media site. I saw a lady I met once on the site. I knew she was a minister.

"I don't know what you are doing right now" I said to her, "It is best you stop doing that and minister to me!"

She did and lead me back to the Lord. I told you the Lord will send people in at unexpected times and in unexpected places to minister to you. I want to encourage someone with this. If you have been contemplating suicide and you Know, when, where and how you are going to do it. Compel someone to listen now!

I divorced and married the co-worker we lived together three years. This was wasted time.

A Broken Cycle

My co-worker had become wife # three. The relationship was destined to fail. The only thing we had in common was our profession, and a physical relationship. It reminded me of Samson and Delilah. Once, while I was supposed to have been hers she turned on me. That is when I knew I was in Satan's trap. They used deception and lies to keep me abated.

Some people end up being speed bumps in your life. They bring on so much adversity that they slow you down enough that you cultivate a relationship with the Lord Jesus that would not have come by any other way. You end up praying more and harder, if you ever have had a relationship with God.

This relationship was a plot from Satan. She systematically dismantled me. It started with emasculation. Emasculation- Deprive a man of his role or identity. I would cook and clean because we both worked and it was simply not being done. I stepped it up and took on the task. When I did, we would have the biggest arguments for no reason. She would instigate the fatal blows.

She turned to pornographic material as if to say I was not man enough. She would spend all nights on pornographic websites. I would walk by the bathroom and hear her pleasuring herself. Intimacy with us was not happening. Satan's ploy was to draw me back into pornographic trap through her. Intimacy with us only came with a stipulation. I had to view pornographic material with her first before we could proceed. I found out they had been involved in some extra activities outside the marriage. The Holy Spirit showed a person she was involved with. I asked and she admitted he asked her but she turned him down. A sure sign of infidelity is when the things you have always done are not good enough anymore.

Change Must Come

This relationship was getting worse. Some incidents were fringing on violence. She was speaking of doing violence to me and playing the crazy card. She spoke of killing me. This relationship was growing worse by the minute. I wanted God to help me then! I knocked myself but was caught in the common cycle of man; sin, retribution, repentance, restoration, and rest. I was in the repentance phase. I was finally on the verge of transitioning from retribution, getting what I deserved or brought on myself. I needed help. I wanted help.

Here is where I missed it. I thought God was going to reach down from heaven and move things all round. I thought He was going to fix things.

Finally, one night we were lying in bed. She said, "I want to ask you something."

I gave her the platform and these words came out. "I'm bored with you, this relationship, our intimacy and our marriage!"

I asked very simple question. "Are you still in love with me?"

She said, "No!"

At that point, the doors of my heart slammed shut. I could not let her back in or have access to my heart anymore. I did not have anything else to give this relationship. I put up with her stealing from us with getting cash advances off my credit cards, and funding gambling habits. On top of this all, she pawned her wedding rings.

Still, I was asking God to deliver me from this situation. It did not dawn on me I had to do something. I had to make a move.

Finding Courage

I found the courage to move. I left my house like a displaced refugee. I have been seeking the mandate, mission, calling, and ministry that supposed to be operating in my life ever since. Lord I am all in.

Paul encourages us to fight the good fight of faith. It is with the fight of faith against the Devil we win. I have come to realize when you are in disobedience/rebellion you are defenseless. You have no faith or confidence towards God.

It was in these seasons of life I suffered my greatest lost. It was the most expensive time. I endured poverty. Satan took and took. The repo man came, accounts were closed, and deadlines came and went without needs or expectations being met. I was stripped. I was helpless and wondered how much more would be taken.

Satan had knocked me down. He had his heel on the back of my neck. He dared me to get back up. He wanted to see if I had courage to get up and stay in the fight. I realized three things that allowed me to find strength, courage and the will to get up and live.

First, I come to the conclusion I was as low as I could go. From that vantage point, there was nowhere to go but try to come back up.

Second, I had desperately contributed to me coming to this position by (personal pursuit to self-destruction).

Third, I embraced no matter how low I was the position afforded me the opportunity to look up. As long as you can look up you can be delivered.

Jesus is the lifter of your head and the restorer of your soul. I look to the hills, which comes your help.

Your help comes from the Lord. He is the lifter of my head and the restorer of my soul. I found down in the bowels and depths of my being strength and encouragement to get up and fight.

Do you know what else I found? I found Godly sorrow. I found remorse. I found repentance. I found brokenness. I found it was more to this thing than being broken and or my current circumstances or my failings. I was broken because I had gone against the Lord. I failed Him. I didn't listen to His instructions and forced him to deal with my poor choices. It was as a scene from Rocky. I got up and staggered to the middle of the ring where Satan stood. I lifted both hands in surrender to Jesus. He embraced me! I finally, win! All this time, all he wanted was my surrender. He Waited for me.

Twisted Perceptions of Who She is

I would admit I have had some major failings when it comes to some issues in life. To my defense I haven't had any godly positive mentoring. Unfortunately, a lot of what I have learned has been by trial and error. It's been mostly error. One of these areas has been my perception of women. I was taught things I gathered by the men my dad hung around.

1) A woman was a possession of her man.

2) They never to be trusted

3) They are more cunning than men

4) They never sleep,

5) They always plotting

6) They were to be dominated in the bedroom

7) They only based decisions on what pleasures they receive from there lover in the bedroom

8) They are never compassionate regularly , only mean and demanding was norm.

9) They only received respect based on what they do for you. 10) You providing for them is the only sense of you loving them

11) They should never express the things they don' t approve of.

12) A woman crying was a means of getting over. I never heard any of the men say they loved or were in love with a

woman. I perceived it as a sign of weakness if they did.

How could a person establish a lasting, good relationship with these twisted perceptions? The truth is you can't. With this line of thinking I didn' t' !

Holy Spirit Academy

The Lord by His Holy Spirit has to teach you different. But, you have to allow the Holy Spirit to teach you and you learn. This is what He has taught me

1) You must love the very essence of your mate
2) She is a reflection of who you are
3) You are to love her as you love yourself. You have to be to a place where you love yourself first. The Holy Spirit can do this also.
4) You are to nourish and cherish her. (As a tender plant you are trying to see sprout)
5) You are to sow into her development
6) Teach her how to love you
7) Always give her an opportunity to express herself. Even if you don't want to hear it.
8) She is obligated to tell you what's right
9) Always pray her strength in the Lord.
10) Bind up the spirit of discord, spirit of division, and an argumentative spirit.
11) Release peace, unity and joy.
12) Never assume you know how to make her happy.
13) Ask and pray about it
14) Always be gentle and concerned about her emotions.
15) Whatever is important to her let it be to

you also.

16) Be quick to hear and slow to speak.

17) Cover her never expose her weakness or faults

18) Realize she belongs to God

19) Be a good steward over God's property

20) Consider her before yourself in most situations

21) Always be willing to say you were wrong

22) Be quick to forgive

23) Know your relationship is only going to be as good as what you invest in prayer about it . At the end of the day a twisted perception can be transformed into a Godly transition which leads to harmony in Jesus.

Conclusion

I can't really title this chapter the conclusion because my life is yet going on. Thank God! But it is the close of this era. The book of my life is yet open. The latter part of my life is going to be better than my first. I want to leave you with this nugget. God is faithful. He waited for me He was patient in allowing me to get my life in Compliance to His will for me. Believe it or not during all this turmoil people's destiny was going to come out of me coming into compliance to the will of God. Think on this. I was riding down a road one day. I looked out across what appeared to be an empty field. I had driven by this road more than 20 years. I never had seen what I saw this da y. I saw 4 wheelers riding across this same field on a perfectly worn path in the field. I never realized this path was there. Upon closer observation, it was obvious this path had always been there. But, I had not and could not have noticed it was there until I saw the 4 wheelers traveling this path.

By the same token people will never see there is a path that leads straight to God through the person of Jesus. Unless, they see us on the beaten path even when we fall. Get back up and get on your journey. He is waiting for you. Even if you have personal struggles the Lord has need of thee! Through prayer I tried to put these events in chronological order the best I could. But, I found there was a ten year window the Lord done great things through me.

I want to caution people with this never equate fallen with phony. Just because a person falls it does not mean they were never sincere about the things of God in the beginning (before the fall). Jesus is always looking for a way to use you. Let me give you a case and point. During the ten years I was turmoil free the Lord used me mightily. Demons were casted out of people, throat cancer healed, liver cancer healed, blindness healed, tumors dissolved, aneurysms healed, and women who were not able to carry children to term did.

Yes, I was a Ginuwine Pastor operating in Faith and the gift s of the Holy Spirit. The Lord is faithful to every one of His promises. He will not withhold any good thing if you walk uprightly before him. He cleaned me up and blessed me in one area I could never thank him enough. First, he allowed me to forgive and love my father. He allowed me to lead my father into salvation. He allowed me to pray my father's healing. Lastly, he allowed me to be my father's pastor before he went home to be with the Lord. He was my best member.

God allowed my father and I to reconcile years of differences. I ministered to my father when he needed it most. God will have people in unexpected places at unexpected times to minister to your needs. It was about one year and a half before my father went to be with the Lord. I was called. They had rushed him to the hospital. They said he had four aneurysms and they wanted to operate on him.

I came in the ER filled with the Holy Spirit. I said, "You are holding resentment and un-forgiveness because your biological father walked away. You are holding un-forgiveness and resentment against your half brothers and sister because you believe they worried your mother to death!"

He said, "Yes!"

I said, "You got to let that go!"

He said, "Ok"

I said, "Tell God you forgive and let that go."

He told God just that.

After a few days they let him come home. He told me when he forgave and I prayed for him, Jesus came in the room.

Jesus said, "Everything is going to be alright."

Even unbelieving doctors had to admit they did not know how he made it.

He told his story everywhere he went

until God called him home. The victory in his death was this. Dad showed me how to live and die as a man of God! It was most powerful lesson he ever taught me. He waited for my father. He waited for me and He is waiting for you!

My dad asked me to forgive him for not giving me the best upbringing.

I let my dad off the hook.

I told him, "You did the best you knew but God finally gave me the dad that I always wanted."

Then I told him something that I never had said before, "I love you, Father."

The End

Made in the USA
Columbia, SC
06 October 2023